T0381397

Come to Him in the Silence; Meditations for Life's Journey

GREG LARDY

WestBow Press books may be ordered through booksellers or by contacting:

WestBow Press
A Division of Thomas Nelson & Zondervan
1663 Liberty Drive
Bloomington, IN 47403
www.westbowpress.com
844-714-3454

Interior Image Credit: Greg Lardy

ISBN: 979-8-3850-2419-3 (sc)
979-8-3850-2420-9 (e)

Library of Congress Control Number: 2024908139

Print information available on the last page.

WestBow Press rev. date: 05/29/2024

WESTBOW
PRESS®
A DIVISION OF THOMAS NELSON
& ZONDERVAN

Dedication

This 30 day devotional is dedicated to my family.

The love and grace they have shown me provide inspiration for this work.

Foreword

"Lord, teach us to pray…" (Luke 11.1). The Lord invites us to pray. How do we pray? There are so many forms of prayer. Over the years, people have shared how difficult it is to engage in prayer. "How do I get started? I don't know where to begin!" This devotional is for you.

This inspiring devotional is a wonderful aid for us to pray. We live in a world filled with noise. We are challenged to follow Jesus' example of going away to a quiet place for prayer. To hear God's voice, we need to seek a few moments of silence each day. This book can help us to meditate and pray.

Come to Him in the Silence: Meditations for Life's Journey is designed to allow the reader to hear God's voice by reading a Scripture passage followed by a short reflection. It contains pictures of nature that can draw us to the beauty of God's creation.

Greg Lardy, the author, has written this devotional for people like him. He is an active lay person that fills his day with the responsibilities of family life, demands of his job and fulfilling his mission to serve the Lord in his parish and beyond. He has discovered what a gift it is to make room for a period of silence and experience the presence of God.

"But when you pray, go your inner rom, close the door and pray to your Father who is in secret. And your Father who sees in secret will reward you." (Matthew 6.6)

Rev. Phil Ackerman
Holy Cross Catholic Church
West Fargo, ND

Preface

This book began as a few social media posts during Lent several years ago. I wrote from the heart about my faith life and from those few posts, this effort began. The devotional I was reading at the time noted that men typically don't share much about their faith lives on social media and it challenged the reader to share a few things on social media throughout Lent.

Once the Easter season concluded, I was ready to move onto something else but several people who had been following my journey throughout Lent encouraged me to keep going and to keep sharing. Before I knew it, I was sharing a daily inspirational message! The encouragement to do this helped fuel a desire to go deeper with my relationship with God.

As part of the devotional, you will note several photos that display the beauty of creation that I have experienced. I often find my time in nature a time to draw nearer to God and I hope the photos in this devotional are also a way for you to see God in the things that surround you.

It is my sincere hope that this devotional will help you draw closer to God by spending some quality time with Him each day. In today's busy world, a few minutes of silence each day brings clarity, draws us closer to God, and allows us to better understand His plans for us.

Acknowledgement

Thanks to Paul, Katrina, Prakash, Katie, and the many others who have continued to encourage me to write this devotional. They saw value in it at the outset and continued to remind and encourage me to see the process of creating a book through to the end. A special thanks to Ellen Crawford, the talented professional who edited this manuscript. May she rest in peace.

Introduction

We are all seeking something. The wants and longings which we have stem from our innate desire to have a relationship with God. It is my prayer that you find this devotional a way to draw deeper into your relationship with God and that it inspires you to seek the silence that is required to hear His voice.

DAY 1

Colossians 4:2

Devote yourselves to prayer, keeping alert in it with thanksgiving.

· · · · ·

The hardest part of anything in life is starting. Whether it be a new routine at the gym, a new job, a big project at work or starting a good habit. Anything that requires discipline will seem difficult at the start. It takes dedication and patience to have it become a habit.

Watch anyone who is a professional athlete, musician, artist. They did not get to be a professional at their craft overnight. It took countless hours of practice and dedication to get to be a professional. It is work that we never see as casual observers. We look at them and are jealous because they make it look easy, but what we don't see is all the times they tried and failed. We don't see all the time they put into practicing, working out, developing skills and studying.

So it is with our own prayer lives as well. We need to be disciplined for prayer to become a daily habit. God desires a deeper relationship with each of us. That happens when we set aside time each day to be with him, listen to him and converse with him. It requires discipline and dedication. Don't be discouraged at the start because it may seem difficult. Stick with it and good things will happen.

DAY 2

PSALM 46:10

Be still, and know that I am God! I am exalted among the nations, I am exalted in the earth.

· · · · ·

Being in the present is very hard for us to do. We are constantly thinking and worrying about what we have coming up later in the day, tomorrow, next week, next month, next year. Or we are frustrated about something that happened in the past, bothered by something someone said, perhaps angry that we were cut off in traffic, or irritated about some other minor inconvenience.

God desires a relationship with us that is in the present. He desires a small bit of our time on a daily basis to help us get to know Him. He desires to give us time that is free of worry and anxiety about the future and time that is free of irritation, frustration and anger over what might have happened previously.

So don't be afraid of the silence. The silence is where you will find Him seeking you. The silence is where He will calm your fears about the future. The silence is where He will give you peace from the frustrations of the past. The silence is where you will get to know Him.

Day 3

EXODUS 14:14

The Lord will fight for you, and you have only to keep still.

. . . . .

When we take time to be in silence and to quiet all the other noises and distractions in our life, we begin to know ourself. Our worldly culture has so many distractions and noises. The noise is constant. The noise prevents us from hearing the whisperings of our soul.

Quiet and silence allow us to hear and understand the very essence of our legitimate needs and desires. But we also begin to learn more about areas that we are being called to grow, areas where we have weaknesses and areas we need to leave behind. And sometimes we don't want to know and understand these things about ourselves.

We have to be deliberate in seeking silence. We have to learn to turn off the distractions, the noise, the commotion. In the silence, the very essence of our being is revealed. In the silence, we can make peace with the past, cast aside anxiousness and worry about the future, and focus on the present.

Day 4

1 Kings 19:12

And after the earthquake a fire,
but the Lord was not in the fire; and after the fire a sound of sheer silence.

· · · · ·

ur world will try to deliver all sorts of messages to us that are incongruent with the truth. One of the simplest ways these messages are delivered or the truth is hidden from us is noise. The world seeks to deliver enough noise in our lives that we become confused about what is important.

Noise drowns out the truth in many ways. In some situations, noise comes from being so busy we don't take the time to seek the truth or enjoy the stillness. In other situations, the noise comes from us stubbornly refusing to be still long enough to give the still, small voice a chance to be heard. In other situations, we become prideful and think we have the answers or the answers we are given are not palatable from a human standpoint. Sometimes the answers require sacrifice of time, pleasure or worldly possessions, so we refuse to listen.

No matter the reason, noise serves as a distraction. Noise is a mechanism that prevents us from hearing and receiving the truth. We need to make way for a few moments of silence each day. To seek the quiet stillness that allows us to hear the still small voice.

DAY 5

MATTHEW 25:16

*The one who had received the five talents went off at once
and traded with them, and made five more talents.*

·   ·   ·   ·   ·

The parable of the talents reminds us that we have all been given unique gifts. How we use them and develop them is up to us.

It is important that we take time to understand what our talents are and what gifts we have been given. Have we taken the time to listen to how others have encouraged us? Have we sought time in silence to listen to what God may be telling us about our gifts and his plans for us?

Talents and gifts are revealed gradually and, through time, we come to better understand how we might use them in the mission that lies before us. It's up to us to listen and then to begin to develop and multiply those gifts.

DAY 6

LUKE 4:42A

At daybreak he departed and went into a deserted place.

• • • • •

uke's Gospel (Luke 4:38-44) describes the scene in which Jesus heals Simon's mother, who was suffering from a fever. Later that day, many others who were sick or afflicted came to him for healing. Once he had healed those people, he left for a "deserted place."

We need those deserted places. Away from the phone calls, emails and busyness of life. We need to seek the silence that allows us to recharge. That allows us to hear the still, small voice that guides our actions.

We live in a world filled with noise and clutter. A world filled with things that society thinks are important. But we need to seek time away from those distractions to be whole.

DAY 7

1 JOHN 4:18

There is no fear in love, but perfect love casts out fear;
for fear has to do with punishment, and whoever fears has not reached perfection in love.

· · · · · ·

One of the things that holds us back in achieving what God has in mind for us is fear. Fear is the greatest killer of purpose.

When we are fearful, we fail to act. When we are fearful, we shrink. When we are fearful, we don't speak up. When we are fearful, we are complicit in our silence.

What happens when we overcome the fear we encounter? We stand up to the bully. We speak out for the oppressed. We act with kindness and mercy. We no longer worry about what others may think. We act with bold confidence.

Day 8

Proverbs 4:23

Keep your heart with all vigilance, for from it flow the springs of life.

. . . . . .

As a scientist, I have been trained to answer questions, solve problems, develop solutions. But some things cannot be answered with the mind.

At various times, we must follow our heart. Going where the heart leads and trusting in the little whisper we hear in the wind or the gentle urgings tugging at our soul sometimes will mean that people will say that you are not being logical or that you haven't thought it through.

At these times, you will be required to have courage and faith: courage to continue on the path, to look for the gentle reminders that you are following your heart, and faith that God is leading you, that you are headed in a direction he wants you to go. Take time to listen and discern what you are being called to do. It will be there in the silence.

DAY 9

1 SAMUEL 3:4

Then the Lord called, "Samuel! Samuel!" and he said, "Here I am!"

· · · · ·

In the First Book of Samuel (Ch. 3), we hear the story of Samuel being called by the Lord while he was sleeping. Samuel gets up and goes to Eli, telling him, "Here I am, you called." Eli tells Samuel to go back to sleep because he did not call him. This happens three times before Eli realized that the Lord was calling Samuel.

How many instances in our own lives have we been called but have not known, understood or had the courage to answer? Maybe the call is drowned out by other distractions or noise in our lives. Maybe we don't recognize the voice. Maybe we choose to purposely ignore the call.

Being prepared to answer the call requires us to be still and be ready to speak the words that Samuel spoke the third time the Lord called. "Speak, Lord, for your servant is listening."

It requires us to be in the quiet places to hear the call. It requires us to have the courage to respond back, inviting the conversation to begin. It requires us to have the faith to respond to the call.

DAY 10

HEBREWS 13:5

Keep your lives free from the love of money, and be content with what you have; for he has said, "I will never leave you or forsake you."

. . . . .

Our society, especially Western culture, places a great deal of emphasis on materialism and consumerism. If you turn on the TV, listen to the radio, open the newspaper or have access to any other form of media, the messaging is clear: "Buy this item and you will be happy." "You need this to be happy!"

The list of items is endless. The marketing messages subtly make us feel like we will be unhappy or be left out if we don't have this item. The messaging tells us we won't be part of the "in group" if we don't have this item. The problem is, the happiness we get from these things is only temporary. It doesn't last.

We have to be able to move past the consumerism, see past the marketing messages, and begin to seek things in our lives that do bring peace, joy and happiness. Finding true happiness is not going to happen by amassing more furniture, cars, boats or other things.

Experiencing joy comes with finding our mission, understanding our role and being countercultural. It means learning to share our gifts and blessings with others who are less fortunate or don't have the basic necessities, not with closets, basements and storage units full of material things that we don't really need.

Day 11

Mark 4:3

Listen! A sower went out to sow.

· · · · ·

The Gospel of Mark (4:1-20) describes the parable of the sower and the seed. Many of us have heard this parable countless times in a variety of settings.

Listen carefully to the very first and the very last words Jesus said to the crowd as he was on the boat teaching them this parable. Do you know what it was? The first and last words he said were, "Listen!"

In all the times I heard this passage, I had not thought about the word "listen" being the first and last thing he said. How often had that word been something I disregarded or skipped over?

Losing the nuance of these parables is so easy with all the noise that is going on around us. We are busy thinking about things at work, about something I have to do later in the day or later in the week. We're too busy worrying about something in the future or frustrated over something that happened earlier.

All those things reduce our ability to listen. We are unable to cut through the noise and find the meaning. Noise distracts us and we are unable to listen.

Finding just a few minutes for quiet reflection can help us to discern the voice speaking directly to us. If we really want to listen, we need to find the quiet. We need to seek the stillness.

DAY 12

PSALM 25:4

Make me to know your ways, O Lord; teach me your paths.

. . . . .

We are going to have times when the path that we are traveling is not going to be well marked. It will be confusing. It will seem as if a thick fog is surrounding us and we have a hard time making out the road signs.

I believe these are the times when God is asking us to trust Him and to take the time to truly listen for His counsel in our lives. That counsel may come in the form of a friend or mentor who can offer guidance or has had experience in the particular area that is not clear to us. It may come in the form of simply finding some quiet time to spend meditating on what God may be asking us to do or asking the Holy Spirit for guidance with a difficult decision.

When we encounter these situations, getting frustrated can be easy to do. We want the path forward to be clear. We want to know exactly which direction to go. But remember that God wants us to place those anxieties and worries in His hands, to offer them up as a means of learning to have greater faith, to have patience as we find our way.

Day 13

MATTHEW 6:19

Do not store up for yourselves treasures on earth,
where moth and rust consume and where thieves break in and steal.

. . . . .

Deep down inside, we each have a desire to know God on a much more intimate level. That hunger, that calling is present in each of us, but there are times when we mistake that hunger for something else.

There are times when we attempt to replace that hunger and that call with more material goods, more power, more of something the world has to offer, rather than seeking God and offering Him that place in our lives. The challenge with any of these things the world is offering us is that they fail to satisfy. They cannot compete with what God is offering us, but we have been conditioned by society to believe that they will. Society tries to convince us that these things will be more satisfying, but over and over again we discover that this is not true.

The hunger we each have for God begins to be satisfied when we order our priorities to be more in line with what He is asking from each of us. Giving Him some time out of our busy lives, listening for His call, seeking Him in the solitude. When we begin to do these things, we will discover things that bring us peace and joy. We will discover what His plan is for us, what role He is asking us to play, and what we can do to make this world a better place. Then we will be able to start satisfying that hunger.

Day 14

JAMES 1:14

But one is tempted by one's own desire, being lured and enticed by it.

·   ·   ·   ·   ·

At times, our lives are going to seem like they are out of tune. In music, this is called dissonance. If you've listened to dissonance in a musical piece, you almost can feel the tension and strife that is within the music. Our lives can feel the same way when things are not going well.

Many composers purposely build in dissonance into their music, however, because it allows them to ultimately resolve the chord. To bring it into harmony. To make it sound beautiful.

Our lives are like that, too. Dissonance is present because something is not quite right. Perhaps our relationship with those around us is amiss, perhaps it is how we are spending our time. Whatever the reason, when the composer helps us bring it back into tune, beautiful things happen.

Don't fight the dissonance. Listen to it. Realize what it is. Seek the one who can resolve the chord.

DAY 15

PSALM 32:8

I will instruct you and teach you the way you should go; I will counsel you with my eye upon you.

. . . . .

If you listen to the messages from our culture, you often will hear things that emphasize our individual choice and freedom as being of the utmost importance. Choice and freedom are important. But one of the subtle underlying themes in these messages is one of "I." I am most important. It is my choice.

These messages diminish the importance of discernment and discovery of what God has planned for us. We mistakenly think we need to write our own story, to go through life on our own as a fiercely independent manner.

God calls us to trust him, to seek his wisdom and counsel as we discover his plans. These plans may not be what we originally have planned for ourselves. But if we can step away from our pride, we will discover that all He has in store for us is good and He has riches waiting for us beyond measure.

Day 16

MARK 9:24

Immediately the father of the child cried out, "I believe; help my unbelief!"

· · · · ·

If you listen closely to many passages in the New Testament, Jesus is calling people to trust him. He is pointing to areas in their lives which require trust in God's plan.

It is easy for us to worry. There are plenty of things in our lives that can cause us to be anxious or worried. Things at work, things at home, natural disasters, national news, international events. The list goes on and on. The news is full of things that somebody else thinks we should worry about.

You know what? God didn't write those newspaper articles and He didn't write the script that the news anchor is using. But He did inspire four people to write the Gospels. The Gospels tell us not to worry about tomorrow, not to be anxious about what might happen. The Gospels tell us that we are to trust in Him and in His plan. The author of life is telling us not to worry or be anxious.

What areas in your life require more trust? God is calling you to take that step. He is calling us to give those worries to Him and to trust Him completely.

Day 17

REVELATION 3:20

*Listen! I am standing at the door, knocking; if you hear my voice and open
the door, I will come in to you and eat with you, and you with me.*

· · · · ·

We live in a culture that is constantly trying to shape and mold us into the ways of the world. This occurs in subtle and not so subtle ways. Whether we know it or not, the media, the music we listen to, the people we spend time with all mold and shape us.

At the same time, God stands ready to transform us. But He will not do it alone. We have to invite Him into our lives. In a sense, we have to partner with Him in the work of this transformation.

One of the ways to begin this process is to simply make the invitation. Ask Him to begin the process. Ask Him to take one area of your life and begin the work of the transformation. If you ask and give Him time, He will begin. But we have to make the invitation.

Day 18

Genesis 28:15

Know that I am with you and will keep you wherever you go, and will bring you back to this land; for I will not leave you until I have done what I have promised you.

· · · · ·

There are many times when God seems far off, distant and even aloof. I'm not sure why that happens or what it means.

Sometimes it happens when I'm tired or have been working long hours and when the challenges seem large. Sometimes it happens when things are going well and there are few problems.

I do know that whether He seems close or far, He is still there. I just need to be patient and trust that He is there and that He is listening. I need to continue to go about my prayer routine, maybe change things up a bit, and continue to seek the places where I hear His voice. In nature, in a quiet church, in a beautiful sunrise.

Day 19

MATTHEW 9:9

As Jesus was walking along, he saw a man called Matthew sitting at the tax booth; and he said to him, "Follow me." And he got up and followed him.

. . . . .

In the Gospel, there are many times when Jesus invited others to join him by saying something like "Come, follow me!" If we are watching for them, we will see that in small ways, we are getting that call on a daily basis as well.

The question becomes if we are really listening for it or if we are too busy with other things to actually hear it. The busyness of our everyday lives often prevents us from hearing that message. In some cases, we hear it, but we are afraid to act on it because we are afraid of what others might think of us.

The ability to listen and the courage to act on this call to follow him will lead us into a deeper relationship with him. The opportunities will present themselves in many small ways if we are ready to listen and willing to answer him.

DAY 20

MARK 7:35

And immediately his ears were opened, his tongue was released, and he spoke plainly.

. . . . .

Mark's Gospel (Mark 7:31-37) describes Jesus working a miracle with the deaf man who had a speech impediment. Jesus opened this man's ears to hear and removed his speech impediment.

In our lives, we often experience times when we fail to hear God speaking to us. We want to follow our own path. We dismiss the voice of the Holy Spirit speaking to us, pushing us to make a decision that, deep down inside, we know is the right decision. For a multitude of reasons, we tune out that still, small voice or we simply refuse to hear it.

It takes courage on our part to truly listen and then act on what we hear. Sometimes it takes a miracle for us to hear those words. God is speaking to us each and every day, whether we are listening or not. It's our job to listen.

DAY 21

PSALM 13:1

How long, O Lord? Will you forget me forever? How long will you hide your face from me?

• • • • •

There are many times in my life when God seems distant and far off. There are times when I don't feel as if He is listening.

When I look back and reflect on those times later, I can see that He has been there in the form of people who have helped along the way. In the form of a phone call from a friend. In the form of a note of encouragement or the smile of a stranger.

There are times when we become so engrossed in what we are going through that we don't look up and see or can't look up and see how He is working in our lives. If you are in one of those time periods in your life, just realize that He is there. He is working through the actions of others who care deeply about you. He is walking along side you, even though you may not be able to see it.

Day 22

PROVERBS 27:1

Just as water reflects the face, so one human heart reflects another.

· · · · ·

We often go looking for the incredible in something that we only experience once in a lifetime. I think we need to look for the incredible in the everyday. We miss out on so much each day because we get lulled into thinking that the things we do every day are mundane, routine things that have no meaning. The things we do every day can have the most meaning if we look for it and are open to it.

The incredible happens when we have an unexpected conversation. When we truly listen, don't judge, and are open to hearing what people are concerned about. The incredible happens when we take the time to notice the beauty around us. The incredible happens when we take the time to appreciate the little things that we have been blessed with. The incredible happens when we are open to having the incredible happen.

Today, look for the incredible in the ordinary. Look for something wonderful that has been right under your nose. Look for those opportunities to experience the everyday in a new way.

DAY 23

ACTS 9:3-4

Now as he was going along and approaching Damascus,
suddenly a light from heaven flashed around him.
He fell to the ground and heard a voice saying to him,
"Saul, Saul, why do you persecute me?"

. . . . . .

We don't often take the necessary steps to truly encounter God in our daily lives. There are many times when we are not listening and not seeing what is going on around us. And what is going on around us, especially in the lives of those we interact with, is part of how we likely will encounter God on any given day.

We mistakenly think that the encounter will be something like Saul experienced. Being knocked to the ground with a bolt of lightning. That might happen to us, but we are much more likely to have the encounter be a much more subtle experience.

Are we truly present to those around us? Are we listening to what they are saying? Are we observant enough to know when they might be hurting? When we truly see and hear, can we respond with empathy and compassion to what they are dealing with? And we, in turn, become an instrument of God's love for them.

Day 24

PHILIPPIANS 1:9-10

*And this is my prayer, that your love may overflow more and more
with knowledge and full insight to help you to determine what is best,
so that in the day of Christ you may be pure and blameless.*

. . . . .

It is easy to get frustrated or discouraged when it seems like God has not revealed His plans to us. As a society, we have become accustomed to having everything we want available almost instantaneously. This expectation for instant information does not fit the way God reveals Himself and His plans to us.

Discernment and understanding God's plan requires us to be patient and accept His timeline. The plans He has for us are revealed little by little. Take time to pray and to reduce the noise and distractions so we truly can listen is what is required of us.

By asking God to reveal our hearts, talents and unique mission that He has in store for us, we will see it revealed. Don't become discouraged when it does not happen on our human timelines. Seek the quiet, still places where He will speak to you.

DAY 25

PSALM 62:5

For God alone my soul waits in silence, for my hope is from him.

· · · · ·

Do you really know what you want? Most people don't know what they want because they really haven't spent the time thinking about what it is they want. They haven't taken the time to discern what they want or they avoid the question entirely.

How do we find out what we want? In almost all cases, this comes about from spending time in the classroom of silence. It comes from listening to the small inner voice that tells us what is most important to us. It comes from deliberate acts of discernment meant to uncover what is truly important and what we were created to be. Silence, thought, listening: Those actions will reveal what we want more than anything else.

Day 26

PROVERBS 14:17

One who is quick-tempered acts foolishly, and the schemer is hated.

· · · · ·

We often find ourselves being reactionary. Little things can set us off. We may feel like we have a short fuse. Worse yet, others around us definitely notice we have a short fuse.

How do we deal with this or find ways to manage it? When we take the time to find and appreciate silence, stillness and solitude, we can face the situations and problems we encounter in a calm manner.

Silence, stillness and solitude have a calming action. The time we invest in the silence each day pays dividends by allowing us to calmly face situations and not overreact.

Day 27

---

1 Thessalonians 5:21

But test everything; hold fast to what is good.

. . . . .

When you have a decision to make, do you ever look for that quiet space? Do you seek a place away from all the noise? The noise in our lives adds to the clutter and confusion in our minds. It prevents us from getting clarity.

Even something as simple as turning off the radio in the car and driving to the store or to work with no distractions can be helpful. The quiet helps bring the problem you are trying to solve into focus. It helps you clarify what you believe to be important and allows you to focus on your principles.

Decision making, thought and problem solving oftentimes require moments of quiet, of silence and of solitude. These moments bring the issue into focus, allowing us to see potential solutions that we may not have thought of or consider other pieces of information that we may need to make a good decision. And they allow God to speak to us if we are willing to listen.

Day 28

LUKE 18:39

Those who were in front sternly ordered him to be quiet;
but he shouted even more loudly, "Son of David, have mercy on me!"

. . . . .

The Gospel of Luke describes the story of the blind man begging by the roadside as Jesus and a crowd approached (Luke 18:35-43). One of the nuances in the story is that the man was rebuked by people in the crowd and they told him to be silent.

How often do we act like the crowd, discouraging or drowning out other's prayers because we are mean spirited, judgmental or uncaring? Are we taking steps to lift one another up when we have the opportunity?

How often do we become easily discouraged in our own prayer life? Do we let the noise and the hustle and bustle of everyday life drown out our cries to Jesus? Do we silence our prayers because the crowd (materialism, societal pressures, our broken world) discourage us into thinking that God will not hear our prayers?

One of the lessons from the blind man is to continue to pray with faith and not let our prayers be drown out or silenced by the crowd.

DAY 29

MARK 7:29

Then he said to her, "For saying that, you may go - the demon has left your daughter."

. . . . . .

The story of the Syrophoenician woman (Mark 7:24-30) coming to Jesus to ask him to drive out a demon is, in part, a story of a parent whose persistence in prayer was rewarded. She was not going to take no for an answer and, ultimately, her prayers were heard.

As parents, we spend a lot of time worrying about our children. Some of those worries are minor, others are worries about much larger problems that they may be facing in their lives. It's reassuring in this story to know that Jesus answered this mother's prayer because she was persistent. She did not give up.

We can definitely learn something from this interaction. In persistence, this woman sought out Jesus, she found him when he did not want to be found (he went to this house to be alone; v. 24). We can be reassured that in persistence, we continue to build faith, even while our faith is being tested. In persistence, we learn that God provides. In persistence, we learn that God listens to even strangers (remember this woman was not of the house of David; she was a foreigner). In this story, persistence definitely paid off for this woman. We can all learn something from that example.

Day 30

LUKE 18:6-7

And the Lord said, "Listen to what the unjust judge says.
And will not God grant justice to his chosen ones who cry to him day and night?
Will he delay long in helping them?"

· · · · ·

The Gospel lesson of the story of the persistent widow and the unjust judge (Luke 18:1-8) contains important revelations for us related to our persistence. The widow is persistent, trusting that God will ultimately deliver a just judgement for her and knowing that God only wants what is good for her. The judge ultimately renders a just judgement for her, even though he "neither fears God, nor respects any human being."

Part of what this parable is about is the need for persistence. When people are persistent in any endeavor, it brings about good fruit. Persistence and the willingness to keep at a task, project or activity eventually yields positive outcomes.

Another facet of this Gospel reading is the necessity of patience. The widow was patient with God, knowing that eventually her prayers would be heard. She had faith that in due time, she would get her reward. She trusted that in time her prayers would be answered.

Many of you likely have things on your prayer list that have been there for a long time. Don't give up. Be persistent. Have patience. Trust that God will answer your prayers on His schedule.

About the Author

GREG LARDY grew up on a ranch in southwestern North Dakota and developed a love for ranching, agriculture, and the outdoors there. The oldest of five boys, his parents modeled for him a deep faith and trust in God. His professional career has been spent working in agriculture and higher education. He and his wife, Lynae, reside in West Fargo, North Dakota. They have three children and six grandchildren. In his free time, Greg enjoys reading, running, biking, and photography.

If you would like to learn more or enjoy daily devotionals,
you can follow the author on social media:

Facebook: Greg Lardy

Instagram: greg_lardy